THE WINTERING KUNDALINI

SASENARINE PERSAUD

THE WINTERING KUNDALINI

PEEPAL TREE

First published in Great Britain in 2002
Peepal Tree Press Ltd
17 King's Avenue
Leeds LS6 1QS

ISBN 0-948833-79-3

CONTENTS

SECTION I

SECTION II

SECTION III

SECTION I

NO NEW WORLDS

A dribble of colour,
Slightly yellow tears
On summer trees
Tell it all.

Here I would want to stop
But you remind us
There are evergreens too —
We're not
We're not
Unchanging

Finally
Even as you do
I'll make a pre-emptive strike
Before *The Charioteer* can finish his dialogue
That the living's already dead
You'll know this new
Is old as new.

BUT FOR THE O OF ALL, HERE OR THERE

This we know –
I know
Here or there
There or here
A crow's a caw
A caw's a crow
A crow as beautiful a bird
As any.

This we know
I know
Monster or genius
Picasso or Matisse
Genius or monster
Wife or woman
One is both and both
One
I gave you all –

Not the all of all
But the O of all,
Zero of nothingness yet is all.

And so we know
I know
Here today
Or here tomorrow
The leaves grow greener
As we speak
And as we sleep
The trees grow greener
In the dark this night
In the light of morning –

This we know —
I know
Tonight the leaves are black
And yet are green
And tomorrow is now
And never
You I and I you
Not the all of one
But the O of all

This we know
O this we know —
I know . . . !

MEDITATING ON GANESH IN A SNOWSTORM

Normally, I have a *trishul*
that day they gave me sword
Naag neck,
While Ganga made love to Jammuna
On my head

O *Parvati,* Kaha hai?
Descending
And this boy would block my
Way when that day
They gave me sword
He didn't know
He didn't know
Why or how the dark head
Darkened on the ground of
Clotting blood.

Outside it swirls, whirls
Snow doesn't dog or cat
But the elephant of all seasons
And time, it snows the
White elephant

Did I go for sex
Dispensing knowledge, testing
Cutting edges of *Dharma?*

Who knows

What these whimsical minds pretend
Make real.
That day they gave me sword!

COMINGS AND GOINGS

Winter wags his scaly tail
Knowing his time is near.
Pain on the tip of mine twitch
Like the stumped tail of a sheep
Or doberman –
The time is near.

What if this is the second
Or third coming
What if I search and sift endlessly
Like old women 'picking' rice
before the wedding?
If your coming could save me
I would be a whore waiting,
Dreaming and waiting on my back.

To sell my body to save my soul!

But comings?
Goings matter most.
Only I can save myself
And you yourself.
Aham Brahma Asi
Aham Brahma Asi
I am he, I am he.

And yet I will miss you
Who calls so quietly at my door
Who goes . . .

SPEAKING WITH THE LEGS OF LIGHT

Ah, you have been waiting,
You and you and you
And I —

But it couldn't be
for sun was always there
And it couldn't be
for heat was always there
Even in the cold.

And having waited through
Dark months
You bring out legs —
The light of limbs have come
To dissolve the dark —

But do they meet
Ever?
And do we know?

I have long thin beaks,
A little curved with learning.
It doesn't matter from where
I've come
It's where I'm going.
It doesn't matter what manner
of birds
have been humming since darkness
jumped out the mouth of light —
Petals are not enough
It's nectar we're after.

When will you bring your legs
out of its darkness –
Only darkness melts with darkness,
Don't you know?
You and you and you
And I,
The not-I!

Around the Zero
they sit and stare
at the black O
The nothingness of everything –
A circular pool, its multiple pissing penises
in the public, concrete-heart of
man cannot escape himself?

Women shed cluttery shoes
And bare their toes
to the legs' escapable heat;
Sun O shining sun
Quickly, come quickly from above
with your piercing gleam
and powder-brown my body!

I could, I would
like the flung away shoes
And flung away skirts,
The flung away thighs,
Bare my slitting O
To sunned circular;
Memo:
That circled Zero's empty
Has it all, content
and uncontent are erect
ejaculating sprouts!

But rows of penises in the circle centre
And on the ringed stairs
like mini-amphitheatres we sit
In summer lunches
In stolen breaks
Watching and waiting
Waiting and watching
For the drama proceeds
For the days pass
gladiators –
In offices speculating on numbers!

And Sunya, Sunya the Zero –
Number of all numbers
Will not buy a car
dwells here
And so we come
And stare at aloneness,
Push our legs for borrowed brownness
Bury our heads in sap of books
Fence words of love on work
Taste the tongues of other countries –
Whom are we fooling?

The penis pissing on the air,
Pissing on water,
Might be that frothy song
enchants
hope spatters on water
spatters on drying faces . . .

Who knows
Who wants to know
Why dogs lie on mats in the sun
And smirk at the frustrations of their
Masters!

THIS LONG WAIT

Time slips hurriedly through
Trembling fingers
Words miscegenate
Organs unwind to aging
Hearts tick
Swifter than the Demerara.

You'll remember green
hearts loaded mid-river
For foreign ports
Still valuing wooden toes
Or wooden knuckles
Sticking into salty brains
Picking memories;
A cleaner mud
A living trunk
A tree
Would slip from primal being,
The logger's saw
This ripping time
seeps quickly through quivering fingers –
Hurry, hurry the clock . . .

And yet like stainless steel *stambh*
(in Delhi's courtyard)
Rustless wait for whom
For when
Existence is unciphered
You wait
And seem to know for certain
(I don't)
The clock will never stop

So still my fingers stumble
And still
Time slips swiftly through . . .

COBRA IN THE BASKET

Revisited
But a little late in the day
– cold and dark we called it night –
No voice rattles in my rusty throat
Do
And more Do
Think
and no-think.
In the circled serpent's
Puffed hood,
Invisible tapered tail,
Slow walks will not do on unswept streets
Hips hooded, skin stretched to sex . . .

But retreating to the hole
The wicker basket's silence
Waiting.
Waiting . . . until the master
Lips his flute
And music calls
The public call

We perform.

AUDIENCE WITH GOD

Brahma:
Tired of celestial play
I looked in my backyard
and one of my dented childhood
bicycle balls caught my fancy

I thought for a fraction
of creation (equivalent, to say,
all the time Shiva meditated on Kailash)
and from my imagination I sprouted
Trees on Land
Water (actually one bead of salt sweat)
And Aadmi (you'll note that
man here has a female ending —
this should tell you a lot about
who came first forgotten)
And from my mind I made orbit . . .

To make a simple story simpler
for your simple minds
And believable for your unbelieving
Psyches
Aadmi (man) made pins, knives, guns
rockets, robots, bombs, cars from
her/his (and this usage is quite correct) imagination
In time will make praan (life-breath).

And yes,
Set this down
And send this down
We all go empty
of illusions
In the end
In *Kala Yuga.*

THE GURU I

And he said one day,
'I eat no meat.'
And his flesh grew
Smoother than ripe *bigan*
And they marvelled and wondered
At his health.
'But my pupils do
By the daily dozens,'
He explained.

THE GURU II

Who is he whose eyes are stained
by eastern teas
And crystal grains of cane:
Who is he to remain unmoved
by bottoms stretched in bikini-jeans –
Pyar Pukaro (love's call)
rattles all thoughts of dog-sex
Or Mira-love!

Somehow cream slipped in
Somewhat Dutchgirl or Dancow
And tea has lost its green-black
Cane its golden brown
And cream its milk.

And who is he
Whose tea eyes and cane tongue
Having been stained by cream,
Who is he
Can remain oblivious of
the way in between?

THE GURU III

'Do not give a fig
if you have none,' he said
glancing up at the maple
And sitting under its shade.
'First he went to one mastered.
Unsatisfied
he went to the other and mastered
too unsatisfied
he left
And wandered more shrivelled than
A creeper, thinner than a cobra
displaying its fanned head –
And begging his way
Well-fed
He sat like me, but
Enlightened. You would think satisfied.
But no
He would find his former gurus
(for what I would like to ask him)
But they his masters
Were gone beyond him.'

There was silence and she or someone asked
'Why would an Enlightened One
Want to convert the world to his way?'
'I cannot give an enlightened answer,' he said.
And there was laughter and silence after.

Finally it was said,
'The syrup of the maple is sweet
But not sweeter than sweet!'

THE GURU IV

Peeping over the rims of words
The edges of camera lenses
Silence overspilled hedging heads.
Books contain the wisdom of ages
Must be true they knew.
And afterwards
And going outside
And as if reading their minds
He said, 'Rather
       The wisdom of books is in
       The Ages.'

EXIT TO A FAR COUNTRY

Cordelia to the king
Howling in my head –

No hope, no hope
Only sanity of separation
Rain from clouds
Milk from breasts
Mother from son!

Ah, lover and the loved
Reacting to the balm
And poison of violence
In the heat . . .

Sings Cordelia in my head
No hope, no hope
Only the rope of separation
On my neck.

IN THE GARDEN

Dearest, I've not killed Ravan
So we cannot go home.

Has Hanuman deserted me,
And Lanka smokes in my head?

A satellite who would be
a star before its energy's
Burned up in illusion
Records
Lumbering Canadian seagulls
Bombing the ground
Around rundown high-rises
For refuse of poesy . . .

Forgive me, dearest,
For having found Ravan so late.
How he laughs at me
And how my fingers shake,
How unsteady my aim!
How many heads has he! And
Is it the one
That bears my face . . . ?

FIRST BIRDSONGS IN SPRING

Tremulous,
So tremulous in the pin-sprigs
My bones shake,
Old skeletons rattle in revelry
I come
Again
Again

SPRING, TORONTO

Vasant:
Indian spring devolving down centuries
into *Phagun.*
Holika went down in flames
and *Prahalad,* boy-realised,
showing wisdom is not the preserve of age
joined the fray
of colour and fragrance!

Rigged over the *Kaalaa Pani*
so the British Raj
could sweeten European teas
(often Indian tea in European pots)
Indian spring followed
in Phagwah and quite unintentionally
this festival of colours brightened
unaccustomed but soon accepting
eyes.

One hundred and fifty years to move
North – again –
This Canadian spring unimaginable to
tropical eyes:
A hundred shades of green
grass running up discoloured blades,
Shoots afire in 'Holi'-laughing eyes,
A hundred hues of red, yellow, dye
exploding in again-born sky
Again-born eyes!

I understand
in the spring-of-a-twig time
all of one hundred fifty years.
Ah, my Hebrew friends

Two thousand is more than I
can take to make my state
believable!

And yet if another one hundred fifty years
must pass
What difference does it make?

Vasant:
The Vedic spring
This Indian spring
Blossoms again in *Vedic* lands . . .

SHIVA DESCENDS FROM KAILASH

Uncross limbs and open eyes
This dance we wait
This Dha Dhin Dhin Dha
Dha Dhin Dhin Dha
Bharat Natyam and Katak
Should squelch this cold
This much too cold and still
We wait Raag unsung
Before this one last blizzard
Swirled from Samadhi-waking hair.

And while the smiling fire
Transforms ice to blood
And serving flamelets
Sputter likeable reds and blues
We sow seeds from your feet
Dha Dhin dhin dha
Dha dhin dhin dha

And we soak in warmth
A thousand ecstasies of scents
A thousand ecstasies of colours —
These are the thousand headed
Gods the ancients worshipped . . .

Of course, later we will complain of the ferocity
of your dancing
Dha dhin dhin dha
Dha dhin dhin dha
Dha dhin dhin dha
Dha dhin dhin dha
And the heat
And wish for winter —

But now all is gurgling
And full of hope
And graceful Katak

Dha dhin dhin dha
Dha dhin dhin dha

AUTUMN SPIDERS

It is north
And chill.
Spiders prosper in the
Cold:
Silvery webs on bathroom
Corners,
Silvery webs on
Unused doors,
On her corner of the bed
Frosty faced – cold bottoms
Have been growing colder for ages,
Silence: in old age there are
No rapists (battered women shelters and all!)
And cold tops grow
Warmer, colder, warmer worrying
About legalities –
More cobwebbed nearer
Zero degrees Celsius . . .

BETWEEN THE DASH AND THE COMMA

Magnification of a dash
From the north corner
Of South America:
Tons of milky sand
Rising up hills, swaying down
Valleys of untouched timber –
Acres and acres of fertile rainforest
Squatting on the foam-washed solidity
Of South American sands.

Savouring the whirl of a city
North of Ontario
Winter winds whimper for summer.
Cotton balls on evergreens
Cotton fluffs on naked trees,
On hills, on slopes, in valleys
Are a sickly comparison to
Unmelting sands.

But then the spouse's everyday face
Disfigured by sleep and care and worry
Ceases to seem to love!

And why shouldn't the made up face –
The unoften face, the memory-kept
Face always seem to love
If punctuation is reversed?

I can never tell
And so must needs be stuck
Between
The dash and the comma!

Yesterday it snowed again
And it was so beautiful.
In the distance below
Whitewash coated the sprawling city
And the white-dusk darkness
Came so early!
I know you would stare and
Stare as though you were about
To be blinded and this
Was your last sight
And as usual I would cease
To matter being merely
A means to an end

But if you must know
There was a thaw last night
And snow-sperms swam
Into the wombs of lawns,
Somehow a sprinkle of green
Blades twinkled in your
First-time eyes,
The eggy grass lay back,
And in the mid-winter thaw
Spring was conceived!

ABBREVIATED LETTER II

I keep thinking about the politics but
what have I to gain
by electoral surprises . . . ?
Anyway I'm having snap
Breakfast and this is another snap
Letter. You'll remember
I never completed the other and
All your unanswered questions
Prick at my hunger.

Let's see
The trees tout Negroid limbs
(not that there is no beauty —
Black is beautiful too, and
Rushdie must come out of hiding)
For my frozen stare and
I dream of fire-drenched
South American trees
Recall
The fall, the fall was beautiful
But then the fall is always beautiful . . .

The winter wind's a witch
Nothing like our *Sita* of a North-East
Trade coming off the sea —
Faces on trains are whiter
(not necessarily cleaner)
And the sour-perfume-cologne-unwashed
Odour is stronger —
Forgive my diversion

Ah yes, the sun,
But the sun at sun-sit
Is the same god

(*Hay Surya! Hay Bhagwan!*)
The same sun we worshipped
With our thighs touching the warm sea-wall
In the dusk before we left –
Time flies!
And my bus is due
I must compose myself,
I fear I'm still the private person
In a public world you'll always
Know and (I hope) love,
So I must go now if
I'm to keep my something safe.

Always, always
Goodbye.

THE LAST OF THE LETTERS

What have I left to tell you –
All novelty's gone
And having bit exile's apple
Stuck in my throat's
Somnambulistic sleep –
These well meant dwarfs decorate
Their bills, monthly dues:
Here the story ends.

There are no princes/princesses
(we do not need them anyway) here
money overrides and overkills
Though stuck-throat is not stuck brain.
I think and ask unopenly,
Do the red flags fly, my friend,
On strong green bamboo
On new-cut bamboo
Over house, over land
Over dark and interned heads
Mocking democracies of a paraded vote . . .

Ha! Don't fling me communism –
True the *Pandu* shared –
See, *Vajrang Bali* laughs –
My modern *Tale* grows longer
Already I aspire to eyeball *Ravan*
And soon, you know
Soon
I'll have nothing left to tell . . .
The broken soul
The exiled soul may well be like
Shattered pottery – from earth
to earth with water and re-kneading
The long fingers of time

Craft's patient fingers
fashions new goblets –
What wasted masterpieces in museums,
you know the old *kalash* kept our water
so cool as the creek's
sweet only as *OM SHANTI*
        Shanti
        shanti om
        o . . .

And there are no former selves

METAMORPHOSIS

Hurling thought the daytime
Night
Beneath the sound of wheels on
Asphalt
Beneath the downy beds
Of sex
Beneath the seething city
Of seeming
Locked in tunnels of dreams
and penning
Poetry of the under
Ground, poetry of the under
Fed blossoms in the belly
Of the earth –
The foetus of the East
(lately of the South)
Stirs in the womb of the North

Awakens to the loss
Awakens to the winter whirling
Tomb of travel
Tomb of midday night
Tomb of light!

DECEMBER: TABLA AND BHARAT NATAYAM DUET
(a North-South dialogue of sorts)

You would think
Hearing them yearn on T.V.
Radio
A white Christmas is the seventh
Wonder of the world . . .

Roads glistening with
the sweat of rigged elections
Smelling of Black racism's rotten fruits
Rises to disgusted clouds
Rises to disintegrating clouds
Darker than December . . .

Here slushy-soft snow
Crunches nicely under
Tentative steps shamed
in the novelty of flakes'
Sexual dancing to the ground . . .

Sometimes – actually most times –
Gutters choked on discards in heavy rain
And gushed over paves.
Potholes gathered illusive shallowness
And waited for suspicious victims'
Fall and drenching.
The sheltering crowds laughed
Liked spectators in a Roman arena . . .

When I came up from my basement
Just now
I left the dark behind
Of South America sleeping
While the melting snow from cracks

And pave and tree
And drain invites
With a familiar song . . .

It always took a while for
Torrents of water to find the Demerara.
And Main street and Water street
And Crown Street — so many streets
Went under.

We fled to higher ground —

They had started to say
Christ was Black
And god
Was deaf
Or dead!

SECTION II

OBEAH?

When we look into eyes
And mix unspeakables,
When I wrap words and place them
In your heart
Against the evil of separation,
When we spin the charm
Of love-legs to ward
Off dark of lovelessness

We do not even think
Of sorcery!

CHANCE ENCOUNTER

The cone I tasted
Cold on tongue
Coursing down
Water to heart
Is dissipated

In your eyes
The electric gone
Lights of the city
Beckon

The blackout in my heart
Cries hold
I come, I come!

LOST IN THE COLOURS

And this was after that summer —
Just after
And we splashed our colours
I favouring browns and reds
You tending towards yellows and red-whites.
We charmed each other
And I believe all the world with eyes.
Once or twice
We lost each other in the public others
Wondrous chants — 'what colours, what beauty
What love!'
Naturally, before we knew it,
Naked, we were in bed —
And soaked in storms
Snow
Coats of cold fires;
All was subsumed until
Chill opened our eyes.

Nudeness appalled us
And really, in the dark or covered
it was better.
Showers and scents
attempt to hurry spring
A cover-make-over
for skinned illusion.

We forgot, as always
dissolution's easier than creation —
Dressing was painfully longer.

Goodbyes were acrimonious exits
And you didn't even pause for
Wind

Singing softly –
Always down in space
down in time
Present makes past look good
and future makes all look better.

Somewhere, sometime
There'll be another!

IF I MUST FIND YOU

No good god
Not in the spring of conceited
Young buds and blossoms
Or in your winter tiredness
When you shed your healthy defences
And expose your naked needs —
Nor must it be in mine.

If it must be
Then let it be in heat
When all your green senses
Dare my own to logic
But no yesterdays or tomorrows —
No young and unsuspecting,
Old and senile times.

If it must be
Then let it be now!

'MADMAN' ON THE STREETS OF THIS CITY

A girl bends for her dog's shit
and later scoops him from the pave.
A woman straightens with her cradled dog's
wet backside.

These women's ways no stranger than devotion!

Hare Rama, Hare Rama
Hare Krishna, Hare Hare!
Sing saffron robed, shaven
European monks above the fumes
of Mazdas

And dogs of men,
No stranger than themselves;
Training canines to plunge
Through rings of fire
Through tails of illegal trails;
Are leashed.

The bum
Who roams the street
and screams at spirits seen/unseen,
Who's thin, smelly, wasted
On the thighs of summer,
Who suddenly grabs his crutch
And frees his Canaveral cock,
after years learns
He's lost his game.

His play at abstraction's
exposed with flesh.

When woman says it's summer
– and men can we can –
A dog deserts his mistress and
His master.

So a girl scoops up dog
And shit
When she pleases –

Howls the bum to his maddening
Sky –

      All men are dogs, I tell you!
      Dogs to the death of freedom!

LONG AFTER THE AFFAIR HAS NOT ENDED

I

You, no doubt, will be writing poems
More poems soon –
About my heart that went so well under
The tuner's fingers
And better under the player's
And so lovely and so suddenly
Crashes the sitar's burst main string.

It was, I believe, after the audience went
And before they came again for another performance.
Writers should make love to their writing,
Only bodies devoid of baggage should meet –
Once you opened your eyes
Once I saw we saw each other.
'It was a cheap act
Would use all the learned
Notes of the romantic *Raga*
Only to enrich a writing –'
I saw that whisper and did not.

II

'All your poems are a fraud —
(I saw that too)
'Where are *raginis;*
Improvisations make others'
form your own!'
I write a line
(So I lied)
And you two
Earrings dangling from your
blond mess of a mop head.

These lies we lived —
like loving to eternity,
like making a *sada rotie* two
(burst it at the swollen
hot seam in one
in two and two in
one)
like flaking feelings
We have come to believe

really there were no lies,
Eternity came and went
(anything expressible in words is finite)
and we were unprepared.

And she saw again
from another vantage point
Vagina's distended slit –
more like *Zero* –
Was nothing to her yet
her *O* was mother, father
God and goddess of all things
and feelings
and men.

And she heard again from another
Vantage point
Voices to right
Voices to left
Human sounds above
Below
Couldn't touch her
Pipal-tree silence
Appeared like grief.

Finally she said,
'He came for love.'
'For sex,' they said.
'Part of the whole . . . '
'Hole, you mean!' Came their female anger
as she rejoined her beckoning silence
In the early sun shedding rays
like figs, on her head

Like the early morning freshness
her companions embraced
the refuse of night
turned her teary eye
away from that moistened pillow
of a shredded darkness.

THREE BIRDS FLEW FROM A TREE

Rain heaved and tugged,
Nibbled the grass to more
Than a sprinkled greenery.
Some trees were bloody with buds
Others glittered with grains of corn.
But the cold lingered
And for three became unbearable

They shot from their windbreaking evergreen
And startled the others'
Dreams of more colourful times.
One remaining said, 'One will return,'
'Or two,' another

'One having been wounded by one
Hurt the other –
Which one was that?'

And while they waited
Another more ancient, genderless voice
Ventures slowly, 'None will return,'
'None can return!'

And as the months went by
They found the familiar/strange
Genderless voice was correct
And yet they waited
And hoped . . .

Taking turns
They drew long breaths
from rolled and lit tobacco
forgetting fire is as absolute
As god and there are no chosen.
Both burnt fingers and hastened
for other cigarettes
And yet another
As if the bliss of smoke
was forever keeper of sensual
desire, not a ravager of lungs.

Then one day their minds gave up
And they were forever old
And they cursed cigarettes
And said there was no such thing
As smoke.

FROM THIS TYRANNY OF LOVE

Sweet as the juice
of the blackened sugar-cane,
sweet as the pulp
of the uncertain grapes
of common-law domicile
is this journey love.

But one sunless day
your shadow mixed
with the homogeneous dark.
Sun found us in different shades
A false freedom
that you can't go home
again

It's not that 'cane is bitter'
just the tongue succumbs
to fashionable juices
communist/capitalist desires . . .

The road is twice as tough
for the crippled
as for the creeping child.

Ah
Sweeter than your shadow
Is mine
Unhabitable!

BEFORE THE LIFTOFF

And so finally
In the pre-launch hush,
(you to the core of corporate
general staff
and I to humanise the sun)

in our seething catapults of silence
we encode the essence
of our unsophisticated science:
that love is the oppressor's
whimsical payment
for the labouring lover.

For insurance, of course,
we have buried capsules
in the cities of our psyches
so after the inevitable Hiroshima
regenerated selves
will bound to the oppressor's sceptre
from a decoded silence.

APPROACHING THE END OF AN ERA

Aprons fall on sand
Make padding for steps
No. Leave them, love
Let them lie on ancient
shores bashed by ancient
oceans will never end.
There is no curse
No crime in keeping *Murtis*
till we see the higher light
Glitter in your smile

Here
Let us pause awhile.
Take this knife of love
(these strings may hold
You down)
And cut us free
Ourselves unheld by
limbs unhindered by
souls uncluttered by
civilised lines of
Commands —
Just one
When you get there

One incline of fingers
One nod of dismissal
One smile of absolute
Satisfaction with yourself
Will sing to my Soul!

AND THE SOUL MET IN WORDS

To have walked through
Corridors of time unknowingly
Calls for psychoanalysts.

To buy insurance from eyes
Unconsciously produce premiums
Of questions

Souls?
How, when, where?

An accident of motorcyclists
Only then looking at motor
Cycles' damage?

Sure we skipped down
Stairs, skipped up stairs
Of glances
Sure we sleepwalked in daylight
Toward each other unconsciously

But once I opened my mouth
And babbled about blossoms
Of planted saman trees

My soul fell out!

And you opened your mouth
In excited response –

And your soul fell out!

IN A WARM AUTUMN NIGHT

Not yet
Not yet, my love
If you undress your soul
Should it be in winter
When nights are longer
And warmth has meaning?

Tonight the tree
Who first flushed red
In winter yearning
Who turned the hearts of
Summer, the heads of autumn is
defrocked of colour
defrocked of voice

And so early is too early!

Tonight I see
The red berries
The pearly leaves
The white-yellow headlights
Gliding over slithering roads
and this soul snakes smoothly
Hood undone
Heeding the fiery autumn's
John The Baptist fiery speeches
Vibrating your thousand eyes
Thousand ears
So delicately etched in this night's
Slightly mashed
Slightly silver moon!

COBRA: THE WINTERING KUNDALINI

O my love
Doors open
And blades of air
Cut wedges in your warmth,
Dreams coil
Tighter than tendrils,
Space shrinks
Cold climbs higher

Clumsily I try
Tanned boots lined with
A different hair –
Cloaks submerge unmainstream skin.
Oversized gloves prevent
Fingering pens
And scarves of knitted
Sheep swabs my throat.

Finished
You'd think and ready for this chill
Smothered you'd think. ·
Inaccessible nibs, unmoving larynx
Is the song of voluntary silence

O my love
How hot your visit
To my Kundalini's tip
Standing on its cobra's tail,
Your call is unignorable
Your eyes are mine and full
Of light
Your tongue is warm and
Tastes of self

We are the million year
Nagas
Shapes and sizes
Waiting for the millionth night
Your kiss is mine
(a million shapes, remember,
words, or wings or venoms's
all the same)

Your flight is mine
And tastes of love!

FROM KRISHNA'S FLUTE

Not needles etching
Lines on graphs
Or digital jumps
On lighted displays explain
Souls' response to technology;
The deaf hear music
The dumb sing songs
And crippled climb mountained memories
As *basuri,* piano, harp
Sound same
The same, the
Same
Sometimes now, always yesterday
And never
Never any difference in these musics
In our souls . . .

SECTION III

THE DENIAL

Having climbed out of the air
From the green distance
He presented himself:
'What have we got here?' asked the giant
fly – maybe this was ignorance.
The spider spun a little web
A dot of his former self
'What have you done here?' asked the big
fly – maybe not.
'Nothing,' replied the spider honestly,
'I've just arrived . . . '
'It's here that counts . . . ' pronounced the
fly
The interview was terminated

And walking away
He too was scared of
The there
And even more scared of the here
That would deny the There

And when he turned suddenly, he saw the
fly struggling to fly
To the green south
On holiday!

ANCIENT IMMIGRANT TRAIL

Why flaunt your fairer skin
In the summer sky
For browning the summer sun
Agrees with duplicity

I'll leave my turban
In the Punjab
Stop eating curry but
Will you live in *tepees*
Dance around the *totem* pole
Live the eagle ceremony?

Don't ask even
Tell me

Sister
Why pass so arrogantly
On this ancient footpath
Astride your painted bicycle

Have we come from
The place we're headed
And won't I catch you ·
There tomorrow, faceless
Formless, colourless
Companion in this cyclic travel?

The earlier bird catches
The worms of illusion
Perhaps.

THE NIGHT WE FOUND THE ANTI-FUR-CLUB
AT OUR PARTY

Ah, my darling
When we dive in the soft waters
of neon lights around
Soft rock covered with splashes
Of amber algae
And wriggle and twine around
Tendrils of music
What is it we look for!

New forms of sea life?
Sunken treasures from tragic eras
Grimed and silted with corrupting
Times?
Dead fish?

Ah, we surface
In the cold night
The clean air of consciousness
And though we know
We smell of rancid fish
We serve ourselves down to the bone
Convinced it is all for calcium

We feast
Mindless of dead flesh
Dead — deadening fish,
On ourselves
Of ourselves, mindless of cruel
Fishermen's nets.

Ah, my darling
When I bring you furs
To adorn your body, to

Keep you warm from the cold stares
Of humane Societies
Why do you look like the goddess
Of Guilt?

Is it because killing animals
To save their skins is insensitive?
Is it because eating fish is more insensitive
Than the Fisherman satisfying his followers?

Ah, my darling
Let us come out of the soft rock pond
Of sedimental songs
Out into the cold night
The clean air
Of consciousness
Before we serve
All those things
Before we serve
Ourselves . . .

Ah, great poets
Who deride the European gods
As alien borrowed things
In a 'new world' old as any other

Great Poets
Who communicate with ancient
Spirits of Americas
Communicate with borrowed things –
The gods of my parents
Or others' parents, are always
Always our borrowed gods.

Great poets (old – new)
The gods (spirits if you wish) here
Or there are the first colonisers
Whom I seek only to colonise
– then maybe then
I can compare notes on original
Or new world, or
Old world or
Gods!

ABORTION . . . ?

And yet sympathy is selective

For the unseen universe of the womb
We fight a winless war
Abort or unabort
While the living abort their lives
For unaborted hope.

Who cares! Not I
Let the living look after the living
And the dead the dead
I follow illusive essence
Of futures –
Sometimes huff about man in
humanity at the races
forgetting the urban horse
jockeyed by capital.

At any rate I'll never accept
The line beneath
Too simply put

Sympathy is selective
And so is god!

THE CIRCUMCISION

Ah the knife's precision!
(This we do to breeding bulls)
Round and round the lingam
Dances the sharp blades of Yoni.
Blood will rush to muscle the
Instrument's demand for skin's
denuding innocence.

Afterwards, everything is justified.

Lingam stands straighter than phallus
And not even Shiva dares to mark
With knife or skin — fore or aft
No Pandit, Brahmin, Ksatriya
Dares. There's no ringing reservoir
waiting for offered milk
But blood, hot blood
Dried for a perfection.

Sometimes god says through the beards
of celluloid prophets from high on tapering
mountain stone thou shalt . . .
or rather, thou shalt not . . .

But it has been done before
And will, no doubt, be done again
And as we are and are not
All is justified —
Afterwards!

THE GULLS ASPIRE TO BE GAULINGS

And how they bob and weave
Their stumped tails
In a ragged precision of flight
Is not quite right.

And occasionally a brilliance
of one flawless line
From millions confirms the lie.

They left too soon
Or did not want to leave
The womb of creation
And the surgeon performed
Caesarean.
These tails are chopped
And no finely tuned toes
Taper into the infinity of
Not here, not here
Back there, back there . . .

These calligraphic pens
Are bastard sons
The broken nibs-hand-me-downs
Of the lesser sons.

Master pens sway in the middle
ground and exile their flawed
relations to the North or South —
Ah, the centre of their planet
Is warm enough
And knows paradise is not in snow.

Somewhere sing these sketching
Pens —
(Thank heavens, not calligraphic ones)
The enlarged centre of the womb
Is richer, has more knowledge
Than all the heads
The swollen *sinhasana,* the womb
Travels more universes than the toes —
Only that centred whirl makes
heads or toes
Exist, exist.

Swirl and twirl and twirl
The gull can be no more
Gauling than a bird
And yet once a *Ksatriya*
Aspired to *Brahminship*
(and who can be a Brahmin
but a Brahmin!)
And they called him Viswamittra.

Highborn Vasista
Looking up from his balcony
Finally relented.
It is doubtful if they ever understood
But they had to live
Side by side
(the intervening miles inconsequential)

And they did!

That these long summer days
would ever pass . . .
That these micro-waved days
would shrivel and die . . .

Just one look in your eyes
Just one look at your face . . .

If I could lie
In your tropical days
In your Atlantic limbs

If I could be child
Unfutured, child unmemoried
I'd board the plane

But I cannot lie
– ask Henry –
I must justify my act
That long, hot summer days
Are your other breast
which I have yet
to suckle
for your health
And mine!

LOOKING BACK 2

Seagulls
Whirling in the sky
Seeking
Searching from the blue
Scorching summer –

Where are the hand-me-downs
of high-rise people
Where are the immigrant refuse
Flung over balconies –

Aniseed bread
Scraps of sleeping rugs
Tokens contemptuously tossed
With Metro precision?

Ah!
Here
To-ron-to
Men without meaning . . . !

LOOKING BACK 3

Not this thousand-lighted city
in the crawling fall
Not the confusion of naked limbs
Scratching skies and mind
Unaccustomed to northern nudity
Nor Christmas-lighted fruits
Can displace your *Diwali's* eyes . . .

If I were only the little
more oil in your *diyas*
Hugging your earthen bottoms
I'd forget you were *Harijan*
Renamed
For now Untouchable.

LOOKING BACK 4

The gull gawking in my head
In the summer heat
Swerves from the sky,
Hobbles onto the lawn
Of a scraggy Toronto Highrise . . .

This gull too far from Ontario Lake
Is tiger of urban refuse
Tyrant of pigeons
King of survival!

This 'seagull'
Cawing in my head
King away from sea
Merges with and is . . .

Free and free-slaved!

Lottario or lotto
Building-boom speculation
University specialisation
Or simple economy of double jobs –
This city of dreams
And rubber-roaring asphalt
Ravishing unaccustomed eardrums
Rivals rebelling Atlantic on
South American shores.

Ah, but at nights . . .
At nights again
Lives the Cinderella city –
One look from a high-rise
Over downtown before bed
Shows *diya-lighted* runways,
(a headless *Ravan)*
And *Rama* in his *Viman*
Returning to *Ayodhya!*

Raleigh in the tower
MEMOIRS:
A dastardly day, I say
Only yesterday the salt-sweet
Atlantic sprays settled
On eager Elizabeth's bulwarks;
Only yesterday the dark, green
Guianese coastline cooed
Gold and gold
Are waiting gold
And Gold are waiting only
For Europe's Taking!

Ah! Who understood?
The fallen leaves on forest
Floor fluttering brown, unknown
Around in unending golden sun!
I say, I say . . .
At least I brought back pipe
And put IT in and smoke IT —
Don't you all?

Who understood?
Who understands?
why I here in the Tower
Not I, not I

but EL DORADO
O Guiana EL DORADO
I say,
I say old boy just let me go
Just once more . . . !

WHEN THE LAND IS DRY

No my love
It is the land, sodden
Soaked and drugged with water
Which begs the sun
To dry her out,
Open her pores for body cleansing.

Nor does the sun ever hide,
He is hidden
By a deception of earth revolutions,
Moisture sailing in the sky
And the land lost in ecstatic motion.

No my love
The rain never leaves the
Land dry and parched,
It is the land who drains
The water from her breasts
And powders herself with dust,
It is the land who
Inundated turns her satiated
Face on herself
And lets the water go
And dozes
And sleeps
And forgets!

IN A DARK NIGHT

In the electric gone nights
Of the city
Is the brighter light
The gnawing star
Or blinking candle-fly

Neither
The cat's green eyes
Or the amber dog's

But the continent-hopping
Bengal tiger's burning coals
Staining dark
Stalking shadowy night
Hounding him
To the leap of dawn.

BEFORE GOODBYE:

in heavy rain near the playfields built on the old graveyard

On this road we walk
Between two fields.
Beneath are tombs
We do not see

I know
And history knows
The stench
Is graveyard speciality.

On this road we walk
Around puddles
Of dead water
I tell your laughter

I know
And dead time
Swirling in watery patches
Knows.

THE BLACK ROAD CAME

Once we travelled on water
When the road was a crocodile
Back of holes and slippery
As the *camoodie's*.
Then was no question of inequality
Or suffering but we understood.
In the sun and heat there was dust
So we closed our windows by day.
At night we burnt canefields
Because it was cooler.
At nights we lit kerosene lamps
And stayed away from the flames
Because insects couldn't
Resist annoying flights of joy
To the shaded light
From the secure dark they fled
And fried on kerosene flames.
We shook our heads.

On wet days we opened windows
To no dust – to no road even
And nights saw them closed
On flying ants,
And as there was no road we travelled on water.

And you knew and didn't know
Why
What was done was done
Why
Practicality became commonplace
Why
Commonplace became custom
Why
Custom became religion

Why
Pandits became rebels.

Talk was talk
Until they came
And when they left
Bitumen for an all-weather road
They left their black doubts
And the old red road was gone.
We saw speed and convenience,
The cramped avenues of the cities
More often
Shadows and coloured lights.

We lost the stars,
And didn't mind metropolis'
Lights from polluted skies
Looked brighter

And this was even faster.
Once when we travelled on
Water we were more cautious
More contented.

Now we go faster nowhere
Faster traversing and reversing
Roadway roles (driver and driven)
And as you wish I'll speak
Only for myself:
Drop pretence
Tell it quickly –
We are more equal than our former selves.
Sex is faster
Than its shadows
And faster left behind

Will we never be
Satisfied or contented
Or accepting?
This black road of doubt
Is always beckoning –
Age is no matter . . .
Mind you

I speak only for myself
And I wish
We travelled together
On water.

PORKKNOCKER, COME HOME!

Wildness only in beard.
Malarial eyes condensing
Milk of interiors.
To give is to spend
To spend to give
Years away and return with the gem
Of interior.
In the 'bush' gaudy birds
And macaws soon fly away
Or wither on feeding-poles.

Soon *Hanuman* will fly the sky above
The city
But now it's time for
Sindhoor and thinner milk honeyed
To *Amrit* will sweeten the hole
And the earth itself.
Nowhere is there meat and soon
after the flame crowning the camphor is *taried*
around
Daal will mix with rice and *Bhajee, baigan*
Curry . . .

And maybe some time later
One night when we sit under
The *diya-lit* sky he will talk
Again of the knocking and the pork.

But now he stands in white cotton
Having cleaned the bush from his
Face
Having gone into the barrel
and taken the salt from the meat

And the M from the myth
– wealth is so easily defined –
He stands and offers prayers
And we chant the hymn of ages
OM BHUR BHUWA: SWAAHAA
OOMM BHUR BHUWAA
SWAAH. . .

CONFLUENCE OF DEMERARA AND ATLANTIC

Is this then life,
A hammer of rusted hull
On river, laughing
Woodpeckers' rhythmic
Butting of barks?

A fall of flakes on
Chipping wavelets?

A dance of mud from
Anchor chain down to
Watery partner?

A softly moving motor
A slowly ship
Until the three-sprigged steel
Drifts above salt captor?

No.
This is just a rivered view,
A watered vision!

Beneath the river
Beneath the ocean
There is eternal mother

And above
Around, about the mother
There is the mother/father

One merging in the other.

A PROPHET IN HIS TIME

'Go forth into the world . . . '
he would begin
the silence, staring at a sole
cyclist or pedestrian
Or a gorilla policeman
Aping a farmer
(burnham had just issued another
commandment from his Orwellian cinema –
Each soldier a citizen,
Each citizen a farmer).

The five of us would stare at each
other somewhat laughingly
And catch a glimpse of Atlantic
Waves create fountains on the seawall.
Swallows dived into our souls
Birds floated into the grass of the
Next door YMCA cricket field for
Seeds . . .

'You see Chaucer in his way
Began a written English poetic tradition:'
restarting as suddenly as he had stopped,
the indelibly moist North-East Trades
offering the seed-flower-grass-sea
Scent to noses
And especially the bending thighs
of grass to eyes.

'You have to . . . '
He would catch another glimpse
And stop, at times
Putting on The Cloth and sharing
Wine with us.

In the meantime we blundered on
Blind like January while
May climbed up into the pear tree
And Damyan
'Gan pullen up the smok, and in he throng . . .'
His laughter left us as baffled as his
Sometimes reference
The sometimes sudden deep laughter.

Once a woman came mid-lesson
To make him mortal
But the scars around his neck
Only became legend.

We left blinded Gloucester
on the cliffs.

'You may bring your poems . . . Chaucer . . .'
Lear died before our eyes
And we left for the world.
Once or twice we visited –
It was John or William Street
Where they found him – poisoned
By himself –

We knew alright – though a bit too late
It was the poison of creative genius
Poetics gone with a stare, a look
And neap tide laughter . . .

IN A THOUSAND YEARS

Will the goatsuckers still
Call rainy nights on the Canje
And *Churiles* roll their
Fires further in the forest
And Kaywana's blood burst
Still from between birthing legs?

I wish
And yet I know
Some searching soul
Will stop and see and
Listen and release
My soul
From within her own!

'Meditating on Ganesh in a Snowstorm' p. 12

Naag — Snake. An illustration of Shiva would show among other things a snake or cobra around his head which is a symbol of the kundalini Shakti or power which resides in the base of the spine. The supreme yogi (god?) is one who has mastered the Kundalini and can do anything at will. The trishul or trident in his hand symbolises his mastery over the three aspects of life i.e. creation, sustenance of that creation and dissolution. The stream spurting from Shiva's locks recalls the mythological story of the goddess Ganga, presiding deity of the Ganga (ganges) river who descended from heaven to earth in the Himalaya mountains (Shiva's 'home') via Shiva's hair.

Parvati — Consort of Shiva. In his transcendental periods when Shiva is in Samadhi-bliss in the Himalayas all creative power resides in Parvati (variously known as Uma, Durga, Kali).

Ganesh — Son of Parvati, the lord or god of wisdom often represented with an elephant head or called the elephant-headed god. In Indian mythology the elephant is perhaps the greatest symbol of learning and wisdom. One story of the origin of the elephant-headed aspect of Ganesh states that Shiva after one of his long (years-long) absences decided to come out of Samadhi (the highest form of meditation) to see how life was proceeding. He headed for the abode of Parvati where he was barred from entering by a little boy whom he soon beheaded only to find out from a disconsolate Parvati that that boy was her (and his) son. He soon restored the boy to life giving him the special endowrnent of wisdom i.e. the elephant's head. That boy, Ganesh, became known as Ganapati (lord of elephants, lord of knowledge).

Trishul — trident.

Stambh — Pillar. A pillar of steel unique in the world of metals which has remained rustless over 2000 years. Some historians believe it was erected by the Indian Emperor Asoka (300 B.C.) — at any rate mention is made of it in edicts during the reign of Asoka.

Kala Yuga – Dark Age. In the Hindu mathematical and calendar calculations this present era is known as the iron age or dark age. The scriptures give a day of creation as 4,300,560,000 years. Within this timeframe there are several equinoctial cycles of 24,000 years each divided into spiritually pure, good, not so good and dark periods (golden, silver, bronze, iron ages).

bigan – eggplant (Hindi)

Ravan – Wicked king of Sri Lanka who abducted Sita, wife of Lord Rama, and kept her prisoner in his garden. Rama with the help of Hunaman locates her and after a battle in which Rama slays Ravan they return to Rama's kingdom in north India. Ravan was difficult to kill as he had 'ten heads'– and it was difficult to determine which was the real head. This is one of the main stories of the ancient Indian classic, the *Ramayana*.

'Spring, Toronto' p.28

Vasant – The Sanskrit/Hindi word for spring. Also the Hindu spring festival of colours, variously known as 'Holi' or Phagwah, celebrated on the fifth day (moonlit) in the period of Phagun-Maagh (roughly February-March), the last day of Phagun, first days of Maagh.

Phagun – In the Hindu calendar this is the last month/period of the year.

Phagwah – A type of song sung during the period of Phagun, ushering in the new year. Over the years, and especially in the West Indies, this is the name by which 'Holi' or Vasant has also come to be known. During the Phagwah or 'Holi' festivities (which may last for two weeks – the more pedantic and rigid participants observe the festivities for exactly one week) participants sprinkle and squirt each other with powder of various colours (abrak), a red liquid (abeer, made from dissolving mica in warm water) and perfume – all symbolic of the colours and scents of nature bursting into life after the winter. Groups, families etc. move from place to place 'playing' with each other. Chowtals (lively, vibrant group songs) are sung by groups in procession dressed in white garments, normally a white,

95

unisex loose fitting Indian shirt/blouse called a kurta, somewhat like the 'Nehru tunic' sported by the late Rajiv Gandhi in his trips at home and abroad while Prime minister of India . . . Groups of people in these white garments – flaming with the multicolored powder etc – is quite a remarkable sight. Because it is a boisterous festival many non-Hindus enjoy and participate in 'playing' this festival.

Holika – Aunt of Prince Prahalad in the ancient Indian story in the Puranas. She plays a significant part in the origin of the name 'Holi' – See note below.

Prahalad – A boy prince of ancient India who refused to worship his father, the king, as his father had decreed. The Puranic story goes that his father, Hiranyakashipu, through great penance and prayer was given a boon by god as reward for his great devotion. Hiranyakashipu asked that he be killed neither by man or beast, not inside or outside a building nor at night or day. With the passage of time he felt he was invincible and commanded his subjects to worship him. His son refused saying that there was but one god, Vishnu, and this was a great embarrassment to the father who tried to have his son killed several times always to no avail. Finally it was decided that Prahalad's aunt (his father's sister) would get rid of the boy by holding him in her lap while sitting in a huge bonfire (according to a boon granted her she could not die by fire). When the fire was lit Holika died in the fumes of the fire and Prahalad was unhurt. Hiranyakashipu died shortly after this as god comes out of a pillar in the court yard in the form of half man, half beast (neither man nor beast) who squashes him against another pillar under an arch (neither inside or outside) and it is twilight (neither day nor night). . . *Macbeth*! The influence of the Indian Mythology on Chaucer is documented. Shakespeare, like Chaucer, borrowed from the Europeans (Italians) who borrowed from the Indians via the Persians and Arabs . . .

The night before Phagwah this burning of Holika is reenacted in India and Guyana. Huge Bonfires are lit, symbolic of 'the burning of Holika' – i.e. the burning of evil. Phagwah festivities do not begin until 'Holika' is burnt. This is the 'moral', religious significance of the festival which was later appended to the spring rites. It is also the origin of the name 'Holi' – the Holi festival.

Pani – dark water, associated with the Andaman islands in the Indian Ocean where sepoys (Indian soldiers in British regiments) in the 1857 mutiny were sentenced to life imprisoment, and exiled by the British – i.e. those who were not shot or hanged. A crossing of the ocean by indentured labourers to the West Indies was a dark journey associated with exile to the Andaman. Many sepoys after the mutiny (some British historians call it the Indian revolution as the Indians had set up a provisional government with complete control of North-central and North-East India) was put down changed their names and embarked as labourers for various British colonies. The British shipped 1000 sepoys to Belize (British Honduras) in Central America and work is now afoot to find out about the fate of these sepoys and their descendants.

'Shiva Descends from Kailash' p.30

Shiva – Also known as the Nataraja – literally the lord of dance – both the art form dance and the cosmic dance of creation/dissolution.

Kailash – Mythological abode of Shiva in the snow-capped mountains.

Dha dhin . . . – Notes for counting beats and rhythm in Indian classical dance.

Bharat Natyam – One type of classical dance more popular in south India. This is a very powerful and vibrant type of dance characterised by foot movement and the slapping of the floor by the bottom of the feet.

Katak – literally story. This is a very graceful type of classical dance of north Indian origin, not unlike ballet.

In this poem the dance rhythms increase in ferocity and speed and in the last is slowest again. The speed is representative of the seasons. In winter it is dormant. Fastest in the summer when it is also hottest and mild, slow, lovely in the spring.

Pandu – In the Mahabaharata the Pandavas Princes (the five brothers are also known as the Pandu) while disguised as begging brahmins went to a swyamvara ceremony at which the princess Drupadi would choose a husband. After various exhibitions by the assembled suitors she chose Arjuna, one of the disguised Pandava brothers. On approaching the hut in the forest where they were living with their mother one of the younger brothers excitedly cried out, 'Mother, look what prize we've brought'. To this the mother, without coming out of the hut, replied, 'Whatever it is share it equally' – so they became the five 'husbands' of Drupadi. There are other versions as to how this 'sharing' came about but for years they lived like this, with strictly regulated periods for each of the brothers, until the younger brothers married and she remained with the eldest.

Vajrang Bali – another epithet for Hanuman, worshipped by many Hindus as part of the Godhead, an important character in the *Ramayana* who is sometimes known as the 'monkey-god' because he took the form of a monkey (among others) in the *Ramayana*. As a messenger of Rama he went to Ravan in Lanka seeking the release of the abducted Sita. Ravan had him bound and brought before him in his throne room where he looked on Hanuman from his throne and mocked him. Hanuman promptly burst his bonds and (he was in his monkey form) extended his tail to great length and, making a coil of it several times higher than Ravan's throne, he sat on it as he repeated Rama's request for the release of Sita. Ravan angrily ordered Hanuman's tail set afire and Hanuman, after his tail was lit, flew about Lanka setting fire to all the houses and buildings in the capital – literally burning the capital to the ground before flying back to South Indian where Rama waited near the Indian Ocean.

'Long After the Affair has not Ended' p. 52

Raga (raag) – a combination of musical notes (sa, re, ga, ma, pa, dha, ni, sa etc., which scholars contend are the basis of western music) in the old Indian classical music system to provide a combination which affects the mind. There are 484 Ragas – more than one for each day of the year. Music and mathematics (mathematics, for one ancient school of thought among the Indians, could not be separated from any other aspect of life and was the highest stage of 'expressible' philosophy) are inseparable for many Indians.

Ragini — a composition which allows for great creativity and originality using the basic melodic structure of any raga to create a new variation of that raga.

Sada Rotie — literally simple rotie. There are several kinds of roties. The sada or the simplest is somewhat like a pita bread. When cooked properly it swells like a balloon and it is possible to split it along the seams — giving the appearance of having made two roties from one.

'Approaching the End of an Era' p. 59

Murtis — any representation of god (carving, illustration, painting or object) used by a devotee during worship to focus on the godhead and aid concentration.

'The Wintering Kundalini' p. 62

Kundalini — In Tantric Yoga it is believed that all power lies in the spinal column and anyone able to tap this power makes contact with the godhead and is able to perform extraordinary acts — 'miracles'. Partly because of the shape of the spinal column (like a cobra standing on the tip of its tail) the awareness and 'powers' derived from this type of Yoga are sometimes known as the 'serpent' power. In Indian mythology and religious life the snake is a symbol of divinity and holds a sacred place.

Nagas —snakes. It is believed that some rare cobras (souls working out Karma) can change into any human (or nonhuman) form at will and at a particular time on a particular night in thousands of years (it is believed that this is at the end of each partial dissolution 1/14 of a day of creation — 43,000 human years) a male and female together can break the cycle of dual existence and attain union with the cosmic soul.

99

'From Krishna's Flute' p.64

Krishna — an incarnation of god and main subject of India's most important ancient epic the *Mahabharata*. Krishna is often depicted with a *basuri* (a bamboo flute) and known in this incarnation as the supreme musician. It is written that while still a child whenever he played his flute all animals, birds and people flocked to hear his divine music. Because all the girls flocked to hear his music he and his flute have also come to symbolise romantic love.

'The Gulls Aspire to be Gaulings' p.74

Sinhasana — a seat of learning, especially the sacred seat of the Brahamin. In Guyana only highly respected and learned *Pandits* — (note: my spelling of pandit with the 'a' is deliberate. It is the correct sanskrit and Hindi spelling and pronunciation and this is used in Guyana) sit on such seats during special *yagnas* or on special occasions in *mandirs* (temples).

Ksatryia — generally, warriors, soldiers, protectors, of that caste — the second caste in the 'caste system'.

Brahaminship — of the society of the learned, of the Brahmins. The highest 'caste'.

Viswamittra, Vasista — two of the seven great Vedic rishis — mentioned in the *Rig-Veda*. Viswamittra was born to a Ksatriya family but because of his encyclopedic knowledge and powers he was admitted to the ranks of the Brahmins. Vasista, born to a Brahmin family, at first resisted this but the two men later developed great respect for each other and both were recognised as great Brahmin rishis. This fact, and several similar events, have strengthened the claims of scholars in India (since the earliest times of recorded Indian history) and now around the world that the 'caste system' has largely been misunderstood.

100

'Looking Back 3' p.78

Diwali – ancient Hindu festival of lights celebrated in autumn as a thanksgiving after the harvesting of crops. Later the return of Rama and Sita to their Kingdom after 14 years in the forest and wandering India became associated with this celebration. In anticipation of Rama's return people lighted up the city and the path for his approach. In all probability a 'runway' was marked with flames (diyas) to facilitate the landing of his viman or airbus in which his wife, brother and others travelled from Lanka to the north Indian city.

Harijan – children of han or god. Ghandi in his campaign against the caste system called India's millions of untouchables Harijans.

'Looking Back 5' p.80

Rama – an incarnation of god and subject of India's second great epic the *Ramayan*.

Ravan – wicked and evil king of Lanka (Shri Lanka), once a great devotee of Shiva

Ayodhya – capital of Rama's kingdom in India.

Viman – aircraft or airbus – the art of air travel was known and used in ancient India

'Porkknocker, Come Home!' p.88

Porkknocker – A Guyanese prospector seeking his fortune in gold and diamonds in the vast and rich Guyana interior, northernmost part of the Amazon rainforest system. In the early days the staple diet of these men was salted pork which was transported to remote stations in wooden barrels and as many of these men were often broke between 'strikes' they would scour these barrels for the scrapings hence the term 'porkknocker' i.e. knocking the barrel.

Hanuman – an incarnation of the divine, symbol of strength and victory – the worship of Hanuman and his exploits in the *Ramayan*

are very popular in Guyana and Trinidad. As an ally of Ram he flew back and forth to Lanka. At the conclusion of Hanuman puja, a red flag is raised (usually on a bamboo pole), symbolic of victories; ancient and not so ancient, spiritual and physical.

Sindhoor — vermilion powder applied on a bride's head by the bridegroom, perhaps the most significant act in a Hindu wedding ceremony.

Taried — verb from 'tari', an Indian brass plate used mainly at Hindu ceremonies.

Daal — yellow split-peas cooked like a soup. Very tasty and very popular among Indians and non-Indians in Guyana & Trinidad.

Bhajee — spinach

Baigan — eggplant

Diya-lit — from 'diyas', little earthen vessels lit at dusk on the darkest night of the year (the night of Diwali) to celebrate, in part, the triumphant return of Ram. Diyas are also used in most Hindu religious ceremonies.

Om Bhur Bhuwa . . . —The Gayatni mantra, one of the most sacred and important Sanskrit mantras which is very well known in Trinidad and Guyana where it is repeated during all Hindu religious ceremonies.

Also by Sasenarine Persaud

Poetry

Demerary Telepathy
July 1989, £4.99
0-948833-26-2, 56 pages

Sasenarine Persaud writes with a very conscious sense of Indo-Guyanese ambivalence: an intense attachment to the Guyanese land and a sharp consciousness of the political and cultural oppression of the 1980s. His evocations of landscapes, particularly riverscapes, are immersed in a way of seeing which seeks out correspondences between man and nature, whilst those poems which deal sharply and often wittily with the affairs of state reflect a fear of unbelonging. The poems in the last part of the collection deal perceptively with love and attachment.

'Sasenarine Persaud has ensured that the East Indian element in Caribbean culture is recognized, in poetry at least. Drawing on ancestral memories and imagery and existential experiences, and writing from a distinctive perspective, he affirms the East Indian weft in the tapestry of Caribbean culture... but he is a rooted Guyanese even when he is writing from snowy Canada. Trapped he may be between two worlds and cultures, but he writes feelingly of Guyana's natural environment—rain, rivers, creeks and forests—as a committed belonger. And nature is never described merely for its own sake, but as a mirror of inner consciousness and realities, including love, which he treats with a personal freshness and mature sensitivity. Persaud has to be taken seriously as an "architect of the subconscious" as well as conscious. His is a welcome voice, resonant with philosophy in West Indian poetry.'

Howard Fergus
Caribbean Writer

Fiction

Dear Death
January 1990, £5.99/ US$10.50 /CAN$15
0-948833-28-9, 119 pages

What is the crisis which drives Dalip to question the sources of the person he has become? He senses that it lies in his response to the deaths of some of those closest to him. Growing up in Guyana, he must confront the tensions between the Hindu culture of his family and the Western focus of his education. Should he follow Krishna's counsel not to grieve over what is inevitable or is he denying the full emotional life which his reading of D.H. Lawrence suggests is his human province?

'Love and death seem to be so delicately blended in this novel... a respectable addition to contemporary Caribbean literature which can with justification be selected as a text for formal study.'

The Caribbean Writer

The Ghost of Bellow's Man
November 1991, £5.99/ US$10.50 /CAN$15
0-948833-31-9, 188 pages

When Raj, a reluctant schoolteacher with a weakness for schoolgirls, Hindu activist and would-be novelist, protests against a breach of tradition at his temple, he is confronted by a trail of corrupted power which leads to the heart of the post-colonial Guyanese state. By turns acutely perceptive and self-deceiving, a quirky individualist and a stickler for convention, self-aggrandising and self-mocking, Raj is a dangling man, desperate to create something of value in a shabby and corrupt despotism. Forced to look inwards, he discovers that the truth-telling must begin with himself.

'...poetic in tone, surrealistic in thrust... a good addition to Caribbean literature.'

The Caribbean Writer